50687011492322   2017-03-08 1:33 PM

Lowery, Zoe

Genocide in Armenia

D1709695

GENOCIDE IN ARMENIA

ZOE LOWERY AND JERI FREEDMAN

ROSEN
PUBLISHING

NEW YORK

Published in 2017 by The Rosen Publishing Group, Inc.
29 East 21st Street, New York, NY 10010

Library of Congress Cataloging-in-Publication Data

Names: Lowery, Zoe, author. | Freedman, Jeri, author.
Title: Genocide in Armenia / Zoe Lowery and Jeri Freedman.
Description: New York : Rosen Publishing, 2017. | Series: Bearing witness: genocide and ethnic cleansing in the modern world | Includes bibliographical references and index. | Audience: Grade 7 to 12.
Identifiers: LCCN 2015050449 | ISBN 9781499463088 (library bound)
Subjects: LCSH: Armenian massacres, 1915–1923. | Armenians—Crimes against—Turkey. | Genocide—Turkey. | Turkey—Ethnic relations.
Classification: LCC DS195.5 .L69 2016 | DDC 956.6/20154—dc23
LC record available at http://lccn.loc.gov/2015050449

Manufactured in China

CONTENTS

INTRODUCTION

In 1943, a new term for an old idea was introduced to the world: genocide. Coined by Raphael Lemkin, a Jewish legal professor, in his publication *Axis Rule in Occupied Europe*, it integrates *genos* (Greek for "tribe" or "race") and *cide* (meaning "killing"). So "genocide" refers to the methodical killing of a group of people, such as those of the same race, religion, or nationality. An important element in genocide is that these murders or executions are intentional, or planned. The purpose is to annihilate an entire group of people.

Lemkin approached the United Nations (UN) and proposed a treaty against genocide. He wrote, "The crime of genocide should be recognized therein as a conspiracy to exterminate national, religious or racial groups. The overt acts of such a conspiracy may consist of attacks against life, liberty or property of members of such groups merely because of their affiliation with such groups." On December 9, 1948, in Paris, France, the UN adopted an official position on genocide in the Convention on the Prevention and Punishment of Genocide. The crime of genocide is defined in Article II as follows:

Article II: In the present Convention, genocide means any of the following acts committed with intent to destroy, in whole or in part, a national, ethnical, racial or religious group, as such:

(a) Killing members of the group;

(b) Causing serious bodily or mental harm to members of the group;

(c) Deliberately inflicting on the group conditions of life calculated to bring about its physical destruction in whole or in part;

(d) Imposing measures intended to prevent births within the group;

(e) Forcibly transferring children of the group to another group.

Armenians release doves on April 24, 2015, the one hundredth anniversary of the Armenian genocide, when as many as 1.5 million ethnic Armenians were slaughterd.

Lemkin was motivated by the Holocaust in Germany between 1933 and 1945, when Adolf Hitler and the Nazi Party persecuted and exterminated around six million Jews from all across Europe. Roma (Gypsies), homosexuals, and other minorities suffered and were killed, too. A total of twelve million people died during this time. Tragically, many genocides occurred before this one, and more have occurred since.

The government of Turkey, at the heart of the Ottoman Empire, planned one such genocide. It transpired in the midst of the First World War, between 1915 and 1917. Anywhere from hundreds of thousands to 1.5 million ethnic Armenians who lived in Turkey were victims of this massacre. While a number of Armenians were immediately murdered, some died during forced marches of long distances. Large groups starved and died of diseases during these marches. Furthermore, Turks and the Kurds, tribes who lived in the Ottoman Empire, both attacked them.

One hundred year later, Armenians still remember this horrible time each year on April 24. Under the cover of night on April 24, 1915, the government of Turkey executed a plan it had been making. It arrested more than two hundred Armenian leaders, who were executed. Today, Armenians remember the dead and survivors in communities across the globe.

CHAPTER 1

ARMENIA THROUGH THE YEARS

Turkey's northeastern area has been home to Armenians since ancient times. Their beginnings are in the Caucasus, a region with Turkey to its southwest and Russia to its north. Armenians are a unique race with their own language and culture, including music and dance. Their customary faith is Christianity, with their earliest churches originating in the first century CE. In 301 CE, Armenia officially adopted Christianity as its religion. It was the first country to do so.

Armenia once encompassed land from the Republic of Armenia and Azerbaijan down to the borders of modern-day Iraq and Iran.

The center of the Armenian homeland is the base of Mt. Ararat, a large mountain in northeastern Turkey. Armenia was much larger than it is today. It extended from what is now known as the Republic of Armenia and Azerbaijan south to the Iraq and Iran borders. The country sits in a strategic position. For this reason, it has been invaded many times. At different times in its history, Armenia was occupied by Assyrians, Greeks, Romans, Persians, Mongols, and Turks, among others.

In 1071, Armenia was conquered by the Turks, an ethnic group living to the west. The majority of Turks are Muslims. Hence, religion was a source of conflict for many years before the Armenian genocide occurred. By the 1100s, the Turkish Empire had weakened, and the Armenians were able to establish an independent state again. However, from the 1200s to the 1400s, Armenia was repeatedly invaded by the Mongols, Asian tribes united under warlord Genghis Khan. In the 1500s, a weakened Armenia was divided up between the Turks of the Ottoman Empire and the Persian Empire, centered in present-day northwest Iran. The eastern, Persian part of Armenia was later conquered by Russia, becoming part of the Russian Empire.

A SPRAWLING EMPIRE

At the time of the Armenian genocide, Turkey was only part of the land that was controlled by the Turks. Beginning in 1299, the Turks conquered a large part of Europe, Asia, and North Africa. In addition to present-day Turkey and Armenia, the areas controlled by the Turks included parts of Macedonia, Slovakia,

Hungary, Serbia, Romania, Ukraine, Iraq, Saudi Arabia, Israel, Egypt, and Algeria. Altogether, more than thirty countries were once part of this sprawling empire. The first ruler of this empire was Osman I; therefore, it is called the Ottoman Empire after him. The Ottoman Empire lasted for more than six hundred years, from 1299 until 1922. It lasted so long, in part, because its leaders tolerated different ethnic groups living within its borders, as long as they were peaceful. The empire was broken up following the Ottoman defeat in World War I.

ARMENIANS AMONG THE EMPIRE

Turks ruled the area that had been Armenia from the sixteenth century until the end of World War I. Like much of the world's population during this time, Armenians were mostly farmers. However, they were also active in business, and many held important positions such as bankers and merchants. Being Christians, Armenians in the Muslim Ottoman Empire were never trusted by the authorities. The distrust between the groups dated back many years. During the Middle Ages, for example, the Catholic Church mounted numerous military crusades into the region south of Turkey. Its purpose was to recapture the holy city of Jerusalem, which had fallen under Muslim control. The series of bloody battles left lasting bad feelings between Christians and Muslims.

For the right to live in the Muslim Ottoman Empire, Armenians had to pay special taxes. They were not allowed to testify in court or to bear arms. In addition, they had to pay bribes to local Turkish officials to be allowed to live and work in safety. Armenians also faced opposition from the Kurds, a group living throughout the region to the south and east of Turkey. Despite the bribes Armenians paid, the villages where they lived were often attacked by local Turks and Kurdish tribesmen.

HARSH AND ABSOLUTE RULE

In 1876, Abdul Hamid II (ruled 1870–1909) became sultan (king) of the Ottoman Empire. He was a harsh ruler with absolute power. During his reign, the conflict between the Armenians and the Turks in the Ottoman Empire came to a head.

THE ARMENIAN QUESTION

In 1877, Russia went to war with the Ottoman Empire. The Russians wanted to capture parts of the empire, including the areas that are now Bulgaria, Romania, Montenegro, and Serbia. One of Russia's main goals was to capture the territory known as the Balkan Peninsula, as this would give Russia access to the Mediterranean Sea for trade and military transport. Early in 1878, Russia accepted a truce offer from the Ottoman leaders and signed the Treaty of San Stefano. Under the treaty, the Ottoman Empire ceded key areas of the Balkan Peninsula to Russia.

The western European powers were alarmed by Russia's success in expanding its influence into eastern Europe. Acting together, England, France, Austria-Hungary, Germany, and Italy forced the Russians to accept changes to the Treaty of San

Stefano. As a result, Serbia, Romania, and Montenegro became independent countries, and part of Bulgaria was returned to the Ottoman Empire. The new agreement they drew up is known as the Treaty of Berlin.

The Russians had long claimed to be the protectors of Christian Armenians, and during the war, Armenia was one of the places where the Russians stationed troops. Sultan Abdul Hamid II resented the Armenian support of the Russians. Fearing that he would take vengeance on the Armenians, European leaders debated the best way to protect the Armenians. This was known as "the Armenian question." In the end, the European powers never came up with a good answer to the question.

THE HAMIDIAN ARMENIAN MASSACRES

By 1890, Armenians were becoming fearful and restless with their situation. They began to demand the protections the Ottoman government had agreed to in the Treaty of Berlin. They wanted to be treated equally with Muslims in courts of law, and they wanted to bring an end to the unfair taxation and discrimination that they had put up with. At the same time, Armenians began to express a greater sense of Armenian nationalism, a pride in or devotion to their own ethnic group. In case of armed confrontation with the Turks, Armenian nationalists were being armed by the newly founded Armenian Revolutionary Federation.

Armenians' demands for change were spurred by an increase in education. In the late nineteenth century, many schools had been set up by the Armenian Apostolic Church, to which most Armenians belonged. Also in the nineteenth century, Protestant missionaries from America arrived in Armenia and began exposing Armenians to the American social ideals of liberty and equality. These ideas appealed greatly to the Armenians, who were treated as second-class citizens in the Ottoman Empire.

The first armed clash between Armenian nationalists and Ottoman forces took place in 1894, in Sasun, in northern Turkey. When Armenians there refused to pay their taxes, the Ottoman government sent in Turkish and Kurdish soldiers, who easily defeated the overmatched Armenians.

From 1894 to 1896, constant attacks against Armenians were carried out by Kurds armed by the Ottoman government. These actions were designed to keep the Armenians in line and discourage them from attempting to adopt the European and American ideas of equality and freedom. Armenians' property and businesses were taken from them, and dozens of villages were burned. Between 100,000 and 300,000 Armenians were killed, and thousands more fled the country. This series of atrocities (monstrous acts) is known as the Hamidian massacres.

THE YOUNG TURKS

In response to the oppressive policies of Sultan Abdul Hamid II, several reform-minded Turkish groups had come together back in 1889. They became known as the Young Turks. By 1906, the Young Turks had formed a political party called the

Sultan Abdul Hamid II, pictured around 1900, ruled from 1876 to 1909.

Committee of Union and Progress (CUP). The CUP forced the sultan from the throne and established a parliament with elected representatives. Initially, the parliament included non-Muslim minorities, such as Jews and Armenians. Before long, however, pro-Muslim elements among the Young Turks rose to take control of the party.

AN EMPIRE UNRAVELS

By the start of the twentieth century, the Ottoman Empire was coming apart, as Bulgaria, Bosnia-Herzegovina, and Albania gained their independence. As the empire unraveled, Muslim hatred toward Armenian Christians grew. Because of schools and colleges funded by missionaries, many Armenians were better educated than their Turkish neighbors. As a result, they tended to have better-paying jobs in business and trade than many Turks. In 1909, yet another massacre took place, this one in southern Turkey. Armenians in Adana and nearby villages were attacked, with as many as 30,000 Armenians dying. The cause of the massacre is unclear, but one factor was the rising tide of Turkish Muslim nationalism, fostered by the CUP. A new source of stress was about to be added to the already explosive situation: war had come to Europe, and Turkey was about to become involved.

CHAPTER 2

TURKEY JOINS THE WAR

The First World War occurred between 1914 and 1918. It was triggered on June 28, 1914, when the heir to Austria-Hungary's throne was gunned down by a Bosnian Serb student. Austria-Hungary struck back at Serbia in retaliation. Because major European nations and states had agreements with other European countries, when one country attacked another, all were required to deliver military assistance to one side or the other. Before long, major European powers sided with one of two powers. The Central Powers included Germany, Bulgaria, Austria-Hungary, and countries that were part of their empires. The Entente (*Entente* means "agreement" in French) Powers, or Allies. were made up of France, Britain, Russia, the Italian nations, and states that were part of their territories. The United States initially took a neutral stance, but in 1917, it sided with the Entente Powers.

Early in 1914, Turkey and Germany had signed a treaty agreeing to provide military support to each other. So, when the war started, Turkey joined the Central Powers fighting against the Entente Powers.

ARMENIA'S CRUSADE

Ismail Enver, or Enver Pasha, was one of the Young Turks. ("Pasha" is a title used by high officials in Turkey.) In 1914, he was minister of war for the Ottoman Empire. When Turkey entered World War I, Enver Pasha decided to try to take back the Armenian lands lost to the Russians in the Russo-Turkish War of 1877–1878. On December 22, he sent troops into the Russian-occupied lands, but his army was soundly defeated. Tens of thosands of Turkish troops were killed in battle, and many more died in the harsh winter retreat. There is evidence that the bad weather and inadequate preparation by the Turks played a major role in their defeat. Enver Pasha, however, blamed the Armenians for the loss, claiming they supported the Russians against the Turks.

Ismail Enver, also known as Enver Pascha (pictured here about 1911), went on to organize the Young Turks.

ARMENIA'S STRUGGLE FOR NEUTRALITY

Against all odds, the Armenians in Turkey tried to remain neutral in World War I. But most Armenians in the Ottoman

Empire lived near the border with Russia, the Ottoman enemy. This gave the Turkish government the idea of using the Ottoman Armenians to undermine Russia. Shortly after entering World War I, the Ottoman Turkish government asked Armenians to engage in secret operations across the border in Russia. As a reward for their service, the Armenians would be given additional territory from Russia after its defeat.

For the Turkish Armenians, however, this meant that they would have to attack other Armenians, people of the same ethnic stock and culture. Naturally, the Armenians refused to cooperate. This angered the Ottoman government, which accused Turkish Armenians of being traitors and siding with the Russian enemy. It didn't stop the government from forcing

During the First World War, the Ottoman Turkish government forced Armenians to join the Ottoman army (shown here with German military) and fight for the empire.

Armenians to fight for the empire, however, as 250,000 Armenian men were impressed into the Ottoman army.

In 1914, the Ottoman government began spreading propaganda, or false information, about the Armenians within the empire. The government claimed that the Armenians were in league with the Russians and that they were a threat to the country's security. In light of this propaganda, World War I provided the Ottoman government with the perfect opportunity to rid itself of the Armenian Christians who they had long desired to eliminate.

In 1915, the government issued an order stating that Armenian Christians had to be eliminated. If any Muslim was caught helping Christians, then his or her house would be burned. Then the Muslim, his or her family, and the Christians under the Muslim's protection would all be killed.

THE GENOCIDE'S MAJOR PLAYERS

Ismail Enver, Mehmed Talat, and Ahmed Djemal were the three men who headed the Committee of Union and Progress (CUP). They ran the Ottoman administration during World War I and planned the Armenian genocide. Enver Pasha, minister of war, organized the Teskilati Mahsusa (Special Organization) involved in the Armenian deportations. Mehmed Talat, often referred to by the official title *bey*, was secretary general of the CUP. Talat Bey was the individual who ordered the extermination of the Armenians in the Ottoman Empire. Ahmed Djemal was the third major figure in the planning and

Ahmed Djemal makes sure his troops are in order during World War I. He governed Syria with such viciousness during this time that they eventually rebelled.

execution of the genocide. During the war, he governed Syria, a country bordering Turkey to the south. Djemal's rule was so brutal that the citizens of the area eventually revolted.

The activities of government officials weren't limited to eliminating the Armenians. Some were also war profiteers. War profiteers are people who make large amounts of money from selling scarce supplies during a war. According to a September 14, 1915, article in the *New York Times*, "The inhabitants of Constantinople [the Ottoman capital in Turkey, now called Istanbul] are suffering greater hardships than is necessary, because the Committee for National Defense, run by Enver Pasha, Minister of War, and Talat Bey, Minister of the Interior, has cornered all commodities and is selling them at high prices."

THE "SPECIAL ORGANIZATION"

The Teskilati Mahsusa, often translated as "Special Organization," was established by the Ottoman government early in the twentieth century. In 1913, it was placed under the control of the war department and Enver Pasha. An organization similar to a secret police force, the Teskilati Mahsusa identified and put an end to anti-government activities in the Ottoman Empire. Within the Teskilati Mahsusa, many highly skilled soldiers were trained as special-forces troops. During World War I, they engaged in military operations that were too secret or dangerous for regular soldiers.

The Teskilati Mahsusa was employed to suppress the activities of Armenians, whom the government accused of supporting the Russian enemy. Aided by the Teskilati Mahsusa, groups of Kurdish tribesmen and criminals released from prisons attacked and killed many in the caravans of Armenian deportees.

CHAPTER 3

ARMENIAN ANNIHILATION

Mehmed Talat officially indicted the Armenians of trying to frustrate the Ottoman state's harmony and safety in 1915. The government claimed this constituted a safety hazard to Turks. Because Talat charged the Armenians of working with the Ottoman Empire's adversaries, the government was obligated to take extreme steps to protect the country's stability and safety. Furthermore, it announced an effort to endorse the Armenian population's well being. Therefore, it stated that Armenians would be sent into the central area of the country. Or so it said. This official description of the government's actions was soon exposed for what it really was: Talat's desire to annihilate the Armenians in the Ottoman Empire forever.

Armenian descendants burn the Turkish flag in Lyon, France, to observe the eightieth anniversary of the genocide on April 24, 1995.

In April 1915, preparations for the deportations began. Armenian men in the Turkish army had their weapons taken away from them and were relieved of their duties. Others were dismissed from government positions. Armenian churches were burned and desecrated, and Armenian schools were forced to close. Teachers, writers, and businessmen were rounded up and taken away. Most of them never returned. On April 24, a large number of Armenian leaders and intellectuals were executed. April 24 is now observed by many Armenians as a day of mourning, in memory of the genocide.

AUTHORIZED BANISHMENT

In May 1915, the Ottoman government passed the Temporary Law of Deportation. This gave the government legal authority to deport Armenians at will, simply by declaring them to be suspected of treason. The key element of this law is that it only required suspicion of treason, not proof, to deport someone.

Throughout the empire, orders were sent to police, who began rounding up Armenians. Young men were impressed into the army and sent to the frontlines. Older men were forced to work in labor battalions. They were sent to build roads, carry equipment, and do other labor for the war effort. Poorly fed, these men were worked until they dropped from exhaustion.

In a government proclamation in June 1915, Talat issued a list of rules that Armenians had to follow. Eleanor Franklin Egan, an American journalist, wrote these down in the margins of a book and smuggled it out of the country. She reproduced the proclamation in an article that appeared in the February 5, 1916, issue of the *Saturday Evening Post* magazine. The rules stated:

- All Armenians except the sick had to leave their homes within five days, under escort by armed guards.
- Armenians were forbidden from selling their property or lands they owned.
- They were only allowed to take what they could carry.
- If they refused to cooperate, they would be forced to go or be killed.

Armenian deportees were promised protection on the trip, but this turned out to be a lie. Once the Armenians were removed, all of their property was seized by local Turks and any money they kept in banks was taken by the government.

Armenians were taken from their homes, forced into death marches, and killed during the genocide.

DEATH MARCH

Even the elderly, women, and children were marched away from their homes. Those who were not butchered or shot were deported south to the deserts of Mesopotamia (now Iraq) and Syria. They walked as far as the cities of Aleppo, in Syria, and Baghdad, in central Iraq. For vast numbers of Armenians, the "relocation" turned out to be a series of death marches. They were forced to walk for day after day without food or water, and they were also attacked by Kurdish tribesmen, who killed many and took what meager possessions they had left.

Armenian men traveling with the caravans were usually killed. Young women were often raped or taken captive by Turkish troops or Kurdish tribesmen. The majority of those forced to march from their villages were killed in attacks or died of exposure, exhaustion, or starvation. A 1915 letter from a witness in Turkey states that the Armenians were forced to travel on foot for a month or even two before they reached "the particular corner of the desert assigned to them for their habitation, and destined to become their tomb." The letter also reads, "We hear, in fact, that the course of their route and the stream of the Euphrates are littered with the corpses of exiles, while those who survive are doomed to certain death, since they will find in the desert neither house, nor work, nor food. It is simply a scheme for exterminating the Armenian nation wholesale, … just another form of massacre, and a more horrible form."

In addition, thousands of Armenians in the northern part of Turkey were loaded onto cattle cars and taken by rail to their death. Progress was slow because there was a lot of rail traffic. The trains were needed to move troops and supplies to the battlefront as well. Deportees were often left to wait without food or shelter for days or weeks when the line was backed up, or when the train was needed for other purposes. Even worse, the rail line stopped entirely at two passes in the Taurus and Amanus mountains. Deportees, often shoeless, then had to get off the train and cross the mountain passes on foot. Because of constant delays, concentration camps were established along these passes, with refugees detained for months in horrible conditions.

In 1915, Christian German missionaries wrote to the German government, an ally of the Turks, asking the government to stop the Turkish deportations of Armenians. The missionaries stated that workers on the Baghdad Railway were not allowed to photograph the deportees as a means to prevent evidence of the atrocities from leaking out. Those who failed to turn over photographs would be arrested and prosecuted by the war department. The missionaries themselves were forbidden to give food or help to the starving refugees. If they disobeyed, they were arrested.

Henry Wood was a United Press correspondent stationed in the Turkish capital, Constantinople. In an article published August 14, 1915, he reported:

> *So critical is the situation that Ambassador Morgenthau [the U.S. ambassador to Turkey], who alone is fighting to prevent wholesale slaughter, has felt obliged to ask the co-operation of the Ambassadors of Turkey's two Allies. . . . The position of the Armenians and the system of deportation, dispersion, and extermination that is being carried out against them beggars all description. . . . From eye-witnesses in other towns from the interior, I found that the execution of them was everywhere identical. At midnight, the police authorities swooped down on the homes of all Armenians whose names had been put on the proscribed list sent out from Constantinople. The men were at once placed under arrest, and then the houses were searched for papers which might implicate them either in the present revolutionary*

movement of the Armenians on the frontier or in plots against the Government which the Turks declare exist. In this search, carpets were torn from the floors, draperies stripped from the walls, and even the children turned out of their beds and cradles in order that the mattresses and coverings might be searched.

DODGING DEPORTATION

The majority of Armenians in the Ottoman Empire were deported, but a limited number escaped this fate. There are several reasons for this. First, many Armenians in areas near the Russian border escaped by fleeing into Russia. In some areas of the Ottoman Empire, Armenians were given the opportunity to convert to Islam as an alternative to deportation. Some took advantage of this opportunity, converting rather than facing almost certain death.

Entire Armenian populations of many villages and towns throughout Turkey were wiped out. However, mass deportations were not carried out in the large cities of Smyrna and Constantinople. The government feared that the numerous foreign diplomats and officials living in these cities would observe such activities, leading to objections and international outrage.

Finally, some Armenians survived because sympathetic Turks, Greeks, and Kurds risked their lives by hiding them from the authorities.

Not all Ottoman officials went along with the attempt to destroy the Armenians. Some officials refused to comply, including the governors of Aleppo (Syria), Ankara (Turkey), and Kastamonu (Turkey). For their refusal to cooperate, they were dismissed from their positions. Even some higher up in the government objected. For example, Sheik ul Islam, the sultan's representative for religious affairs, did not agree with the plan. A September 14, 1915, article in the *New York Times* noted that Sheik ul Islam was forced to resign because "he disapproved of the extermination of the Christian elements, against which he protested to the Cabinet."

UNEXPECTED REPERCUSSIONS

Deporting Armenians had a negative effect on the health and comfort of the rest of the Turkish population, too. In many towns and villages, a large percentage of the merchants, doctors, lawyers, and craftsmen were Armenians. When they were all deported, there were not enough qualified Turks to take their place. Thus, the local population often experienced a shortage of necessary goods and services. In some areas where most of the farmers were Armenian, there wasn't anyone left to manage the farms, and crops rotted in the fields. In the immediate aftermath of the deportations, a food shortage struck Constantinople because there were not enough workers to harvest food and get it to the city.

DRIVEN INTO THE DESERT

Deportation turned out to be a very effective way of getting rid of the Armenian population. Often, only a few hundred of the thousands of deportees in a caravan survived to arrive at their destinations in the desert. Those Armenians who survived to reach Aleppo (a city in northwest Syria) or Deir ez Zor (a city in northeast Syria) arrived starving, barely clothed, and without possessions. Ottoman officials did not allow townspeople,

Armenians found some refuge on a French rescue cruiser, but even here conditions were harsh.

charity workers, and missionaries to feed or assist the deportees. From Aleppo, many were moved south to areas deeper in Syria. A great number of deportees were moved east to the desert near the Euphrates River.

All the places to which the deportees were sent had certain things in common. First, they were inhabited mostly by Muslims, who had completely different cultural and religious habits than the Armenians. Second, the locations all consisted of desert, or other terrain that made the region physically undesirable. And, finally, they were far away from the deportees' original homes. To make matters worse, the government dumped the deportees in these remote, inhospitable places without supplies, money, or other support. All the able-bodied men had either been killed or impressed into the army or work groups. This left women and children to fend for themselves or perish.

Thousands of Armenians were held in camps in the Euphrates River valley, Syria, and northern Arabia. A February 1917 article in *Current History Magazine*, published by the *New York Times*, provides insight into what life was like in the desert camps. The writer who visited the camps and observed the conditions wrote, "These unfortunate people are penned up in the open like cattle, without shelter, almost no clothing, and irregularly fed with food altogether insufficient."

ARMENIAN CHILDREN

The relocation marches were especially hard on children. Like the adults, many young people were killed outright. Of those

Armenian children were forced into relocation marches, killed, or orphaned. Some parents gave them to Turkish or Kurdish women to raise, just to prevent them from being killed.

who were not killed, many were orphaned. Others had parents taken away to serve the Turks, leaving the children to fend for themselves. Many parentless children were taken in by Greek, Kurdish, or Turkish families and raised with their own children. Sometimes, local women would approach a caravan as it was passing through and offer to take children from their mothers. Authors Donald E. Miller and Lorna Touryan Miller provide an example of just such a scenario. In their book, *Survivors: An Oral History of the Armenian Genocide*, one survivor recounts the experience she had as a child on the march:

"About this time, Turkish or Kurdish women would come and take children away," she says. "They approached my mother, too. Realizing that there was nothing but death facing us at that point, she gave me to them."

Other children, however, were not as lucky. They found themselves left completely alone, sleeping wherever they could find shelter and surviving on whatever food they could steal.

After the war, charitable organizations gathered as many of the children as possible, placing them in orphanages and trying to locate their parents. After years of living among people of other ethnic and religious backgrounds, many of the children no longer remembered how to speak Armenian. For those children who had forgotten, special classes were held to teach them about the Armenian language and culture. In many cases, it was not possible to locate relatives of the children. However, some were eventually reunited with family members.

Thousands of young girls and women were carried off to become servants or wives of Turks or Kurds who attacked the caravans. Certainly, this was a terrible fate to be taken against their will. However, once they became part of the household of a Turk, they were generally safe from further persecution by the government. In Turkish custom, women take their status from the man of the house. So, a woman married to a Turk is considered to be Turkish, no matter what her ethnic background.

After the war, great numbers of young women and girls fled Turkish harems (women's quarters) and households where they were servants, joining the other young people at the orphanages that offered sanctuary for Armenians. In addition, the British carried out house-to-house searches for Armenian women and children who had been taken by the Turks.

ASSISTANCE

The U.S. ambassador to the Ottoman Empire was German-born Henry Morgenthau Sr. In response to the disruption and hardships experienced by Armenians in the Ottoman Empire, he called on his fellow Americans to provide assistance. A number of prominent people involved in religious and charitable work responded. The Amer-

LEST THEY PERISH

CAMPAIGN for $30,000,000
AMERICAN COMMITTEE
FOR RELIEF IN THE NEAR EAST
ARMENIA - GREECE - SYRIA - PERSIA
ONE MADISON AVE., NEW YORK

The American Committee for Relief in the Near East printed posters in hopes of raising money to assist Armenia, Greece, Syria, and Persia.

ican Committee for Armenian and Syrian Relief was founded, with Congregational minister James Levi Baron as its head. In 1919, an act of Congress made the organization official and changed its name to Near East Relief. The organization gathered volunteers and money from the Armenian communities in America and other concerned citizens. Charitable organizations from several European countries also provided aid. Most commonly, these were missionary organizations. They funneled food, money, clothing, and medicine to the displaced

Armenians in the Ottoman Empire. In addition, the aid workers were a valuable source of information regarding the plight of the Armenians.

When the Turkish government closed the missionary schools that had served the Armenian community, the missionaries who had been involved with those institutions devoted themselves to trying to help the Armenian refugees. However, their efforts were often halted by the Turkish government. Toward the end of the war, the Ottoman government officials became concerned over the bad publicity that resulted from the reports of the horrible living conditions of Turkish Armenians. They responded by cutting off aid from foreign charitable organizations.

CHAPTER 4

GLOBAL COMMUNITY FALTERS

Government officers of the Ottoman Empire did everything they could to make sure evidence of their anti-Armenian activities was kept secret. All private postal and telegraphic correspondence was suspended, whether it was among the capital, Constantinople, and the territories, or between territories. Furthermore, they changed all mail leaving the country, scratching out information they wanted to keep undisclosed. Foreign consuls were prohibited from sending telegraphs in code. Any travelers departing Turkey were searched, and written articles were seized. Nevertheless, intelligence about the brutalities was revealed. Missionaries or humanitarian personnel often reported what they saw when they left Turkey.

So many Armenian men were killed and women carried off that many orphaned children needed help.

INFORMATION LEAKS OUT

Government efforts did not succeed in controlling all of the information flowing into and out of Turkey. Letter after letter from missionaries to their parent organizations told of the fate of the deportees. Reports described how deportees were robbed, starved, beaten, and marched away from villages where the missions were located. Others described deportees arriving at the end of the march barely alive. Missionaries were not the only aid workers to send back word of the destruction. As early as March 1915, the Armenian Red Cross fund had reported to the Red Cross in London that conditions were appalling. One hundred twenty thousand Armenians in Armenia had lost everything, and sources in the region reported that the men were being killed and the women carried off.

Another source of information was the press. Both European and American reporters stationed in the area sent stories back to newspapers and magazines. These articles span the time from the start of the massacres, in 1915, through the prosecution of those responsible at the end of the war. For example, the September 24, 1915, issue of the *New York Times* reads: "500,000 Armenians have been slaughtered or lost their lives as a result of the Turkish deportation order and the resulting war of extinction. Turkish authorities drove the Gregorian Armenians [those of the Armenian Apostolic Church] out of their homes, ordered them to proceed to distant towns in the direction of Bagdad, which could only be reached by crossing long stretches of desert. During the exodus of Armenians across the deserts they have been fallen upon by Kurds and slaughtered, but some of the Armenian women and girls, in considerable numbers, have been carried off into captivity by the Kurds."

GLOBAL REACTION

By April 1915, the reports from Turkey clearly indicated that Armenians were being massacred. It was also clear that more atrocities were likely to occur. As Russia was home to a large

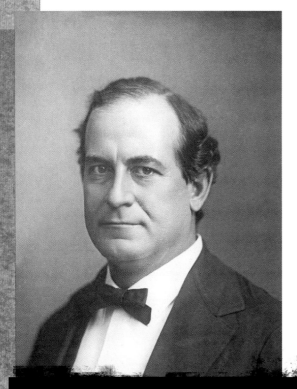

U.S. secretary of state William Jennings Bryan (pictured around 1900), at Russia's request, appealed to the Turkish government to help the Armenians.

number of Armenians, the Armenian Church appealed to the Russian government for help. Russia and the Ottoman Empire were on opposite sides in the war, which made it unlikely that the Turkish government would listen to pleas from the Russians directly. They could, however, work with a country not involved in the war. Prior to 1917, the United States was neutral. So, the Russian government asked the United States to try to get the Turks to stop the atrocities being committed against the Turkish Armenians. The U.S. government agreed. Secretary of State William Jennings Bryan sent a telegram to Ambassador Henry Morgenthau Sr., who was stationed in Constantinople. On April 27, 1915, the U.S. government appealed to the Turkish government to take steps to stop the killing of Armenians.

The following day, Ambassador Morgenthau reported back to Secretary Bryan that he and other diplomats in Constantinople were taking up the matter of the massacres with the Ottoman government. The Turkish government, however, was not cooperative. A short time later, they decided to bar foreign aid workers—a move aimed at reducing the number of reports escaping the area. Turkish government officials told the U.S. State Department that it would not be allowed to send Red Cross doctors or nurses to help the Armenians. In addition, they were barring all other foreigners, including those of neutral countries. Meanwhile, American travelers returning from Turkey in July reported that the deportations of the Armenians were continuing. In response, in October 1915, the United States sent a message through Ambassador Morgenthau to the Turkish government. If the Turks continued to engage in the atrocities against the Armenians, Morgenthau wrote, it would "jeopardize the good feeling of the American people toward Turkey."

German consuls and officials were present in Constantinople and throughout the Ottoman Empire. As the Turks' allies, the Germans were aware of what was happening but did nothing to stop it. Initially, when other countries protested, Germany took the position that it couldn't interfere in the internal affairs of another country. Some countries continued to press it, however. In the fall of 1915, for example, the U.S. State Department asked German ambassador Count Von Bernstorff to get his government to intervene on behalf of the Armenians in Turkey. Finally, in response to increasingly bad international publicity, the German embassy in Constantinople filed a protest with the Turkish government regarding the poor treatment of the Armenians.

On October 6, 1915, Viscount Bryce, former British ambassador to the United States, addressed the British House of Lords (one of the houses of Parliament). He stated that an estimate of 800,000 Armenians killed since May 1915 was quite possible, and that there was "no case of a crime in history so hideous and on so large a scale."

Despite the continued flow of evidence of the Turkish atrocities against the Armenians, the British and American governments did nothing to interfere. Their responses were limited to sending the Turkish government diplomatic protests and requests for a change in behavior. The Turkish government, in turn, ignored them.

According to an article in the *New York Times* published on October 15, 1915, officials of the U.S. government announced that beyond making informal complaints to the Turkish government through Ambassador Morgenthau, they could do nothing further.

Henry Morgenthau Sr. (pictured around 1920) was the U.S. ambassador who took complaints to the Turkish government about the treatment of Armenians.

The plight of the Armenians continued to affect Americans. On October 18, a committee of prominent private American citizens and well-known

Armenians held a protest meeting in the Century Theatre in New York City. The committee was led by Hamilton Holt, editor of the *Independent*, a magazine that had featured many articles about the treatment of the Armenians in Turkey. The committee drafted a series of resolutions, or official judgments, to condemn the actions of the Turkish government regarding the Armenians. While this went on, the Turkish government continued to block foreign aid to the Armenians.

FREEDOM AT LAST!

In 1918, the British crushed the Turkish army in the Middle East. Talat, Enver, and Djemal all fled to Berlin, Germany. Others responsible for the deportation and killing of Armenians abandoned their posts, too. As the British advanced into Mesopotamia, they freed hundreds of starving Armenians. The numbers soon swelled to thousands and tens of thousands of hungry, ragged refugees. In Turkey, a new sultan came to power—a mild-mannered man named Mohammed VI. He apologized for the treatment of the Armenians. Later governments would not be so accommodating.

CRIMES AGAINST HUMANITY

In 1919 and 1920, officials in the post-war Turkish government convened military tribunals to try those responsible for crimes against the Armenians. They believed that Turkey needed to show the world that the country would stand up for justice and human rights. Two of the masterminds of the Armenian genocide, Mehmed Talat and Ismail Enver, had fled the country. Nonetheless, the court tried them in absentia—without their being present. The tribunal convicted Talat and sixteen other leaders for crimes against humanity. Talat, Enver, and Djemal were sentenced to death.

BLACKLISTED

Not all Armenians were willing to let the Turkish government, or even international courts, try and punish the Armenian officials who took part in the genocide. Some members of the Armenian Revolutionary Federation were determined to track down and take revenge on the individuals responsible. They were especially determined to find those officials who had gone into hiding after the war. They drew up a blacklist with the names of two hundred people they considered criminals who had organized the genocide. They then set out to assassinate them. This operation was code-named "Operation Nemesis." Among those they are said to have killed are:

- Mehmed Talat (Talat Pasha), Turkish leader of the CUP, responsible for organizing the genocide, assassinated in Berlin in March 1921
- Behbud Khan Javanshir, organizer of Armenian massacres in Baku, assassinated on July 18, 1921, in Constantinople

- Bejaeddom Shakir Bey, organizer and executor of the Special Committee, assassinated on April 17, 1922, in Berlin
- Jemal Pasha, defense minister, assassinated on July 25, 1922, in Tbilisi, Georgia (one of the countries that used to be part of the Soviet Union)

Defense minister Jemal Pasha (with Enver Pasha) in Syria in 1916.

LIFE AFTER WARTIME

After the war, some Armenians attempted to return to their home villages. However, most arrived only to find that their homes and property had been claimed by Turks or Kurds, or had been destroyed altogether. In most places, the Armenian businesses, schools, and churches had also been destroyed. Basically, there was nothing left of their life before the deportations. Furthermore, although many areas were occupied by Entente soldiers, their numbers were not large enough to protect returning Armenians from Turkish retribution. Often, resentful local Turks attacked returning Armenians and burned their homes. Ultimately, the majority of surviving Armenians left Turkey.

CHAPTER 5

MODERN-DAY ARMENIANS

The United States, Russia, France, and Canada are home to some of the most sizable populations of Armenians today. In the United States, large numbers of Armenians live in New York, Massachusetts, and California. Large populations also live in Toronto and Montreal in Canada.

Hundreds of thousands of Armenians fled the Ottoman Empire during and after the genocide. Even more emigrated after the war, looking for a new life in more hospitable lands. A significant number of emigrating Armenians went to America, where they blended into established Armenian communities in New York City and Boston. Many had immigrated to America in the 1890s, after American missionaries had starting going to Turkey. In addition, a growing Turkish carpet industry had brought Armenian immigrants to the United States. By the close of the twentieth century, the number of Armenians in the United States had grown from 100,000 to 800,000.

TURKEY REFUSES TO RECOGNIZE GENOCIDE

The United Nations has defined genocide as "deliberately attempting to destroy a country or an ethnic, racial, or religious group." The destruction can be accomplished either by killing the members of the group or by putting them in a situation where they experience serious harm. Over the years, there has been much debate as to whether Turkey's actions against the Armenians constitute genocide.

The present-day position of the Turkish government is that it did not commit genocide. Instead, it claims it undertook necessary security measures in a time of war. Even at the time, the Turkish government did not deny the atrocities of which it was accused. It simply declared that the measures were necessary to protect the country against possible attack by a disloyal group. The Armenians, the Turkish government maintained, were a rebellious faction, working against the best interests of the empire.

In December 1916, *Current History Magazine* published information from an interview that the Turkish foreign minister, Halil Bey, gave to an Associated Press representative in Vienna. Halil Bey claimed that the Young Turks had

Turkish foreign minister Halil Bey argued in support of the harsh treatment of the Armenians.

always viewed the Armenians as a valuable asset to the Turkish Empire. However, the Balkan War had led the Armenians to agitate for their own government, separate from Turkey. The Turkish government could not allow this, as the Armenians were not the only people settled in the area they wanted for the Armenian state. Halil Bey claimed that when the war broke out, the Armenians were stockpiling weapons, planning to take advantage of the situation to declare themselves an independent country. He claimed that the only way to stop a nationwide uprising of Armenians was to take drastic measures at the first sign of rebellion. This is largely the position still taken by the Turkish government.

Today, many see the Turkish government's position as not making any sense. If the Ottoman Turks were acting to protect their country in a time of war, why were Armenians deported from all over the empire, even from areas remote from any battlefront? Moreover, why did they deport a vast number of elderly, women, children, and other individuals clearly not engaged in any anti-Turkish military activity?

The question of whether or not genocide occurred has caused difficulties in other countries. In 2006, the French parliament voted to make it a crime to publicly deny the Armenian genocide in France. In response, Turkey cut military ties to France. In 2007, the U.S. Congress was scheduled to vote whether the United States would officially recognize the events that took place as genocide. Armenian communities in the United States had been lobbying hard for the bill. However, the Turkish government was working just as hard to defeat it. The

Turkish government warned President George W. Bush that if the bill passed, Turkey might withdraw permission to use bases in its country for sending supplies to U.S. armed forces in Iraq and Afghanistan. Because of this, President Bush pressured Congress to withdraw the bill in 2007. The bill's supporters may reintroduce the bill later. Twenty-two countries and forty U.S. states have formally recognized the Armenian genocide.

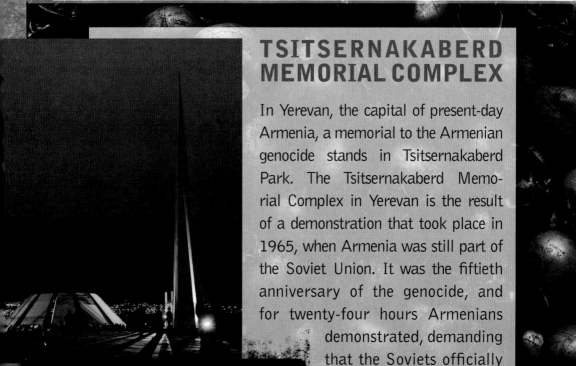

TSITSERNAKABERD MEMORIAL COMPLEX

In Yerevan, the capital of present-day Armenia, a memorial to the Armenian genocide stands in Tsitsernakaberd Park. The Tsitsernakaberd Memorial Complex in Yerevan is the result of a demonstration that took place in 1965, when Armenia was still part of the Soviet Union. It was the fiftieth anniversary of the genocide, and for twenty-four hours Armenians demonstrated, demanding that the Soviets officially recognize the genocide. The memorial consists of a central structure as well as a museum and library.

Tsitsernakaberd Armenian Genocide Memorial stands today thanks to Armenian demonstrators who demanded official recognition of the atrocities.

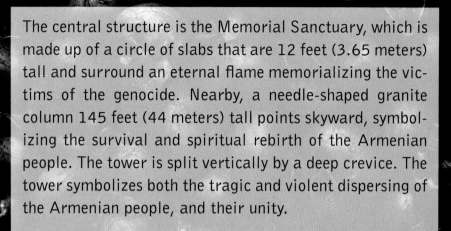

The central structure is the Memorial Sanctuary, which is made up of a circle of slabs that are 12 feet (3.65 meters) tall and surround an eternal flame memorializing the victims of the genocide. Nearby, a needle-shaped granite column 145 feet (44 meters) tall points skyward, symbolizing the survival and spiritual rebirth of the Armenian people. The tower is split vertically by a deep crevice. The tower symbolizes both the tragic and violent dispersing of the Armenian people, and their unity.

THE REPUBLIC OF ARMENIA TODAY

At the end of the war, the Ottoman Empire was divided up by the victorious Entente Powers. On August 10, 1920, Turkey and the Entente Powers signed the Treaty of Sèvres in Sèvres, France. Unfortunately, there was great objection to the treaty in Turkey. The Turkish National Movement arose. Mustafa Kemal Atatürk wrested power from the sultan and set up a new government, turning Turkey into a republic (a type of government in which citizens elect rulers). In 1920, war broke out between Turkey and Armenia. Armenia lost and was forced to give up much of its territory. At the same time, the Soviet Union invaded Armenia, which collapsed and was then absorbed by the Soviet Union.

In 1996, Armenians in the United States and other places in the world took advantage of the opportunity to vote in the presidential election of the Republic of Armenia.

In 1991, the Soviet Union broke up, and on August 23, 1991, the Republic of Armenia declared itself an independent nation. Today, the Republic of Armenia is located between the Black and Caspian Seas. Four countries border it: Turkey to the west, Azerbaijan to the east and south, Iran to the south, and Georgia to the north.

Almost 3 million people were living in Armenia in 2015. Almost 98 percent are ethnically Armenian. The Republic of

Armenia maintains good relations with most countries, including the United States and Russia, although its relations with Turkey are still strained. In contrast to its population of close to 3 million, approximately 8 million Armenians live in other countries around the world, including large communities in the United States and Russia.

In 2015, Armenia commemorated the Armenian Genocide Centennial, or the one hundredth anniversary. Thousands of Armenians gathered together and laid flowers at the eternal flame in Yerevan, Armenia. Others remembered the horrible anniversary around the world. The Eiffel Tower in Paris, France, went dark for the night in honor of these deaths. Rome's Colosseum went dark in their memory as well. In Russia, where a 2010 census revealed that 1.1 million Armenians lived there, doves were set free following a service. In other countries, marches and protests were held to mark the date and express dissatisfaction that justice has not yet been paid. In an article by David M. Herszenhorn of the *New York Times,* Armenian Gevorg Tonoyan said, "Whatever happens, we will not forget. We will come, we will honor our victims, our martyrs."

1889 Groups opposed to Sultan Abdul Hamid II come together to form the Young Turks.

1894 Armed clashes pit the Armenian Revolutionary Federation against the Ottoman government forces in Sasun, Turkey.

1906 A branch of the Young Turks forms a political party called the Committee of Union and Progress (CUP).

1909 Armenians in Adana and nearby villages are massacred.

1913 The Teskilati Mahsusa (Special Organization) is placed under the control of Enver Pasha and the Ottoman war department.

AUGUST 1914 World War I begins; Turkey joins on the side of the Central Powers; looting of Armenian businesses begins.

NOVEMBER 1914 Criminals are released from prison and assigned to units of the Teskilati Mahsusa to kill Armenians.

DECEMBER 22, 1914 Enver Pasha, Ottoman minister of war, attacks Russian-occupied Armenia. His forces lose.

1915 The Ottoman government issues an order stating that Christian Armenians must be eliminated; Armenians are killed in towns and villages throughout the empire.

APRIL 24, 1915 Hundreds of Armenian leaders and intellectuals are executed.

APRIL 27, 1915 The U.S. government begins a series of appeals to the Turkish government to take steps to stop the killing of Armenians.

MAY 27, 1915 The Ottoman government issues the Temporary Law of Deportation, authorizing the transportation of Armenians to remote parts of the empire.

MARCH 29, 1916 The Ottoman government formally rejects foreign aid for deported Armenians.

OCTOBER 5, 1916 The Ottoman government passes a law that allows it to take ownership of all Armenian real estate.

1917–1918 Entente forces take control of important cities in Mesopotamia (present-day Iraq) and Syria; they start gathering displaced Armenians.

1919–1920 Under occupation, the post-war Turkish government convenes a military tribunal to try those responsible for crimes against Armenians.

JANUARY 19, 1920 The Entente Powers recognize Armenia as an independent nation.

NOVEMBER 29, 1920 The Soviet Union invades Armenia, and the country becomes part of the Soviet Union.

MARCH 14, 1921 Mehmed Talat, leader of the CUP responsible for the Armenian massacres, is assassinated in Berlin by Soghomon Tehlirian, a twenty-four-year-old Armenian.

1965 On the fiftieth anniversary of the genocide, people demonstrate and a call for a memorial for the Armenian genocide is finally recognized.

1967 The Tsitsernakaberd Memorial Complex in Yerevan is completed.

1991 The Soviet Union breaks up, and the independent Republic of Armenia is formed.

2015 Armenia commemorates the Armenian Genocide Centennial.

GLOSSARY

affiliation The state of being associated or identified with something.

Aleppo City in northwest Syria.

annihilate To wipe out or eliminate totally; also defeat completely.

Armenian Apostolic Church Christian church to which most Armenians belong.

Armenian Revolutionary Federation Armenian political organization founded in 1890, now an Armenian political party.

atrocity Horrible or monstrous act.

bey Turkish title used by governors and dignitaries.

Central Powers In World War I: Germany, Bulgaria, Austria-Hungary, and Turkey.

Deir ez Zor City in northeast Syria.

deportee Person who is forced to leave a country.

Entente Powers In World War I, the Allies: Russia, France, Britain, Italy, and the United States.

genocide Deliberate destruction of one group of people by another.

indict Officially hold responsible for a serious crime.

intellectual Person who engages in mental labor, such as a teacher or writer.

Kurds Tribal people living in parts of present-day Turkey, Syria, Iran, and Iraq.

Mongols Group of Asian tribes originating in Mongolia and China, united by Genghis Khan.

nationalism Devotion to one's own nation.

pasha Title used by Turkish high officials.

plight Unfortunate or difficult position.

proclamation Official government announcement.

propaganda False information spread for the purpose of harming a group.

war profiteer Person who makes large amounts of money by selling scarce supplies during a war.

Armenian National Committee of America
1711 N Street NW
Washington, DC 20036
(202) 775-1918
anca@anca.org
Website: http://www.anca.org
This organization maintains records, historic information, quotes, and other information related to the Armenian genocide.

Armenian National Institute
1140 19th Street NW, Suite 600
Washington, DC 20036
(202) 383-9009
Website: http://www.armenian-genocide.org
This organization is devoted to the study of the Armenian genocide and offers access to information and photo collections.

Armenian Research Center
University of Michigan–Dearborn
4901 Evergreen Road
Dearborn, MI 48128-1491
(313) 593-5000
Website: http://umdearborn.edu/casl/685096
This center maintains a database of books, articles, and documents on Armenian history and a website with useful facts and information.

International Institute for Genocide and Human Rights Studies
255 Duncan Mill Road, Suite 310
Toronto, ON M3B 3H9
Canada
(416) 250-9807
Website: http://www.genocidestudies.org
This institute promotes the study and publication of information on genocide, including the Armenian genocide.

Society for Armenian Studies
Armenian Studies Program
California State University–Fresno
5245 N. Backer Avenue, PB4
Fresno, CA 93740-8001
(559) 278-2669
Website: http://armenianstudies.csufresno.edu/sas
This society promotes the study of Armenian culture and history, and it publishes a newsletter and journal with articles on these areas.

WEBSITES

Because of the changing nature of Internet links, Rosen Publishing has developed an online list of websites related to the subject of this book. This site is updated regularly. Please use this link to access the list:

http://www.rosenlinks.com/BWGE/armen

Bagdasarian, Adam. *Forgotten Fire.* Paradise CA: Dell Laurel Leaf, 2008.

Balakian, Peter. *Black Dog of Fate: An American Son Uncovers His Armenian Past.* Rev. ed. New York, NY: Basic Books, 2009.

Bournoutian, George A. *A Concise History of the Armenian People* (From Ancient Times to the Present). 6th ed. Costa Mesa, CA: Mazda Publishers, 2012.

Friedman, Mark D. *Genocide* (Hot Topics). Chicago, IL: Heinemann Library, 2012.

January, Brendan. *Genocide: Modern Crimes Against Humanity.* Brookfield CT: Twenty-First Century Books, 2014.

Kheridian, David. *The Road Home: A True Story of Courage, Survival and Hope.* New York, NY: HarperTeen, 1995.

Maybury, Rick J., and Jane A. Williams. *World War I: The Rest of the Story and How It Affects You Today, 1870 to 1935.* Placerville, CA: Bluestocking Press, 2003.

Miller, Donald E. *Survivors: An Oral History of the Armenian Genocide.* Berkeley, CA: University of California Press, 1999.

Morgenthau, Henry. *Ambassador Morgenthau's Story.* Garden City, NY: Pickle Partners Publishers, 2014.

Payaslian, Simon. *The History of Armenia.* New York, NY: Palgrave Macmillan, 2008.

Perl, Lila. *Genocide.* New York, NY: Cavendish Square, 2011.

Springer, Jane. *Genocide.* New York, NY: Groundwork Books, 2011.

Walrath, Dana. *Like Water on Stone.* New York, NY: Delacorte Press, 2014.

Armenian Genocide Museum-Institute. "Tsitsernakaberd Memorial Complex." 2014. Retrieved December 18, 2015 (http://www.genocide-museum.am/eng/Description_and_history.php).

Armenian National Institute. "Armenian Genocide." 2015. Retrieved December 18, 2015 (http://www.armenian-genocide.org/genocide.html).

Armenian Weekly. "Anti-Armenian Sentiment Grows in Turkey." Vol. 73, No. 38, September 22, 2007. Retrieved October 6, 2007 (http://www.hairenik.com/armenian weekly/fpg09220703.htm).

Assembly of Turkish American Associations. "Armenian Issue Revisited." Retrieved October 2, 2007 (http://www.ataa.org/reference/facts-ataa.org/reference/facts-ataa.html).

Bryce, Viscount. "The Treatment of Armenians in the Ottoman Empire 1915–1916." Retrieved October 2, 2007 (http://www.hri.org/docs/bryce/appc_toy.htm).

Ford, Andréa. "A Brief History of Genocide." *Time*, December 9, 2008. Retrieved December 17, 2015 (http://content.time.com/time/world/article/0,8599,1865217,00.html).

Foreign Policy Association. "War Crimes: Armenian Genocide." Retrieved October 2, 2007 (http://warcrimes.foreign-policyblogs.com/2007/04/24/the-armenian-genocide).

Herszenhorn, David M. "Armenia, on Day of Rain and Sorrow, Observes 100th Anniversary of Genocide." *New York Times*, April 24, 2015. Retrieved December 18, 2015 (http://www.nytimes.com/2015/04/25/world/europe/armenian-geno-cide-100th-anniversary.html?_r=0).

Hosfeld, Rolf. "The Armenian Massacre and Its Avengers. The Ramifications of the Assassination of Talaat Pasha in Berlin." Retrieved October 6, 2007 (http://en.internationalepolitik.de/archiv/2005/fall2005/the-armenian-massacre-and-its-avengers--the-ramifications-of-the-assassination-of-talaat-pasha-in-berlin.html).

Miller, Donald E., and Lorna Touryan Miller. *Survivors: An Oral History of the Armenian Genocide.* Berkeley, CA: University of California Press, 1999.

Missionary Review of the World. "Signs of Death in Turkey." October 1916. Retrieved October 2, 2007 (http://www.armenian-genocide.org/10-16-text.html).

New York Times. "Appeal to Turkey to Stop Massacres. Ambassador Morgenthau Instructed to Make Representations on Request of Russia." April 28, 1915. Retrieved October 2, 2007 (http://www.armenian-genocide.org/4-28-15-text.html).

New York Times. "Armenians Dying in Prison Camps. Hundreds of Thousands Still in Danger from Turks, Refugee Fund Secretary Says." August 21, 1916. Retrieved October 2, 2007 (http://www.armenian-genocide.org/8-21-16-text.html).

New York Times. "Defense Committee Corners Supplies." September 14, 1915. Retrieved October 2, 2007 (http://www.armenian-genocide.org/9-14-15-text.html).

New York Times. "500,000 Armenians Said to Have Perished." September 24, 1915. Retrieved October 6, 2007 (http://www.teachgenocide.org/files/Newsaccounts/NYT%20Articles/NYT%20 Article%2)-%20Sept%2024,%201915.pdf).

Peterson, Merrill D. *"Starving Armenians": America and the Armenian Genocide 1915–1930 and After.* Charlottesville, VA: University of Virginia Press, 2004.

RT.com. "Millions Worldwide Mark 100th Anniversary of Armenian Genocide." April 25, 2015. Retrieved December 17, 2015 (https://www.rt.com/news/252909-armenia-genocide-centennial-worldwide).

Stanton, Gregory H. "What Is Genocide?" Genocide Watch. 2014. Retrieved December 18, 2015 (http://genocidewatch.net/genocide-2/what-is-genocide).

United to End Genocide. "What Is Genocide?" 2015. Retrieved December 17, 2015 (http://endgenocide.org/learn/what-is-genocide).

World Population Review. "Armenia Population 2015." September 13, 2015. Retrieved December 18, 2015 (http://worldpopulationreview.com/countries/armenia-population).

INDEX

ABOUT THE AUTHORS

Zoe Lowery is an avid student of history, constantly reading and studying about the past and other thought-provoking topics. She has written and edited a number of books on the topic for Rosen Publishing. Lowery lives in Colorado.

Jeri Freedman has a B.A. degree from Harvard University. She is the author of twenty nonfiction books for young adults, and many of them have been published by Rosen Publishing. Her previous titles include *A Primary Source History of the Colony of Massachusetts*, *Civil Liberties and Terrorism*, *America Debates: Privacy Versus Security*, and *Hillary Rodham Clinton: Portrait of a Leading Democrat*. Freedman lives in Boston.

PHOTO CREDITS